SEÑOR ALCALDE

SEÑOR ALCALDE

A BIOGRAPHY OF
HENRY CISNEROS

JOHN GILLIES

A People in Focus Book

DILLON PRESS, INC.
Minneapolis, Minnesota 55415

Library of Congress Cataloging-in-Publication Data

Gillies, John, 1925-
Señor Alcalde : a biography of Henry Cisneros / by John Gillies.
p. cm. (People in focus)
Bibliography: p.
Includes index.
Summary: A biography of the Mexican-American mayor of San Antonio, Texas, including a chapter in which the mayor offers advice to young people who want to make the most of their education and future careers.
ISBN 0-87518-374-3
1. Cisneros, Henry—Juvenile literature. 2. Mayors—Texas—San Antonio—Biography—Juvenile literature. 3. Vocational guidance—Juvenile literature. 4. San Antonio (Tex.)—Biography—Juvenile literature. [1. Cisneros, Henry. 2. Mayors. 3. Mexican Americans—Biography. 4. Vocational guidance.] I. Title. II. Title: Señor Alcalde. III. Series.
F394.S3C564 1988
976.4'351063'092—dc19
[B]
[92] 87-32456
CIP
AC

Dillon Press, Inc., 242 Portland Avenue South
Minneapolis, Minnesota 55415

Printed in the United States of America
1 2 3 4 5 6 7 8 9 10 96 95 94 93 92 91 90 89 88

Acknowledgments

Many, many thanks to Lila Cockrell, Sister Josephine McGarry, Brother Martin McMurtrey, S.M., Reuben Munguia, Wayne Stark, and the Cisneros family—George and Elvira, Mary Alice, Teresa, Mercedes, and especially Henry—for taking time to talk with me. Additionally, I'm grateful to the Cisneros family for sharing so many photographs; to Barbie Hernandez, Mayor Cisneros's appointments secretary, who arranged for many interviews; and to my Aggie son, Andy, also an urban planner, who helped with comments and suggestions.

Photographic Acknowledgments

The photographs are provided and reproduced through the courtesy of the Cisneros family; AP/Wide World Photos; © 1987 Express-News Corp. (pages 61, 63); John and Carolyn Gillies; Al Guzman (cover); San Antonio Convention and Visitors Bureau; *San Antonio Light* (back cover, pages 70, 88/Jim Blaylock, 93); San Antonio's mayor's office; White House/National Archives; and Oscar Williams.

Contents

Chapter One

The Cisneros House

A photographer shouted from the crowd of national press reporters, "Buenos días, Mayor Cisneros!"

"Buenos días," replied the mayor with a big smile, "and Happy Fourth of July!"

Henry Cisneros, the Mexican-American mayor of San Antonio, Texas, and his family were posing for photographs in presidential candidate Walter Mondale's driveway on that hot July day in 1984. He had been invited to the Mondale home in Saint Paul, Minnesota, to discuss the vice-presidency. The air buzzed with mosquitoes and reporters.

To be considered for the vice-presidential nomination was a "source of honor and pride" for Mayor Cisneros, affectionately known in San Antonio as Señor Alcalde, or Mister Mayor. He was proud because he thought being selected by Mondale as a possible vice-presidential candidate brought honor to his family, his city, and to all Mexican-Americans.

"When my grandfather crossed into Texas from Mexico," Cisneros said, "he could never have imagined that someday one of his own would be interviewed for the vice-presidency of the United States. The fact that this is happening is a testimony to the openness of American society and is proof that if we have faith in people, and give them the tools to work with, they will achieve."

The Cisneros family name goes back to the Spaniards who settled in New Mexico in the early 1700s, nearly a century before the American Revolution. The Spanish government gave the Cisneroses a large tract of land to farm, but as the family grew larger, the property was divided and re-divided until very little was left for each member of the family. Henry's grandfather moved to Colorado to seek a better life for himself and his family.

Henry's father, George Cisneros, was born in New Mexico, but his home was in Colorado. Before Henry was born, the Cisneroses were migrant workers, hired by farmers to work the fields and harvest crops. Many migrant families were constantly on the go, harvesting vegetables in South Texas or Florida, continuing northward, perhaps ending the season picking cherries in Northern Michigan. In a way, the Cisneros family was lucky because they could remain working in the sugar beet fields of Colorado.

In those days, many people were prejudiced against Hispanics, or Mexican-Americans. Henry's father was convinced that getting an education was the way to get off the treadmill of migrant farming and break the cycle of poverty. George Cisneros was the first of his family to complete high school, and after his graduation, he went on to business school, was hired by the government to work in the Indian Service, and became an infantryman during World War II.

He spent nearly three years in the South Pacific and was discharged in San Antonio, where he met Elvira Munguia. She was a beautiful and talented musician who was born in Mexico. George courted her for six months, carefully observing the customs and traditions that applied to Hispanic people who were in love.

After they were married, George and Elvira Cisneros moved into a comfortable house on Monterey Street in the West Side neighborhood of San Antonio. Many Mexican-Americans lived in this old, settled part of the city, some of them in middle-class, well-maintained houses like the Cisneros's home, others in tiny run-down shacks. San Antonio is rich in Mexican-American history,* and is in fact the home of the historic Alamo. "Remember the Alamo!" was the battle cry of 1836, when Mexicans and Texans fought together against the Mexican Army to free Texas from Mexican rule. Today, one-half of San Antonio's population is Hispanic.

Henry Gabriel Cisneros was born in the Alamo City on June 11, 1947. His mother had promised her brother Henry, when he was dying of leukemia, to name her first son after him. Henry's middle name came from Father Gabriel Hentrick, a Catholic priest who was a caring friend to the family during Henry Munguia's long illness.

After Henry was born, brothers and sisters would soon follow: Pauline, George, Jr., Tim, and Tina. Henry has good memories of his family, and describes it as "happy and traditional." In the Cisneros home, as in many Hispanic homes, Henry's father was the head of the household and his mother was the homemaker. The sense of family was very important; the Cisneroses did chores,

*For more information on the early history of Texas and Mexico, see Appendix A, pages 117-119.

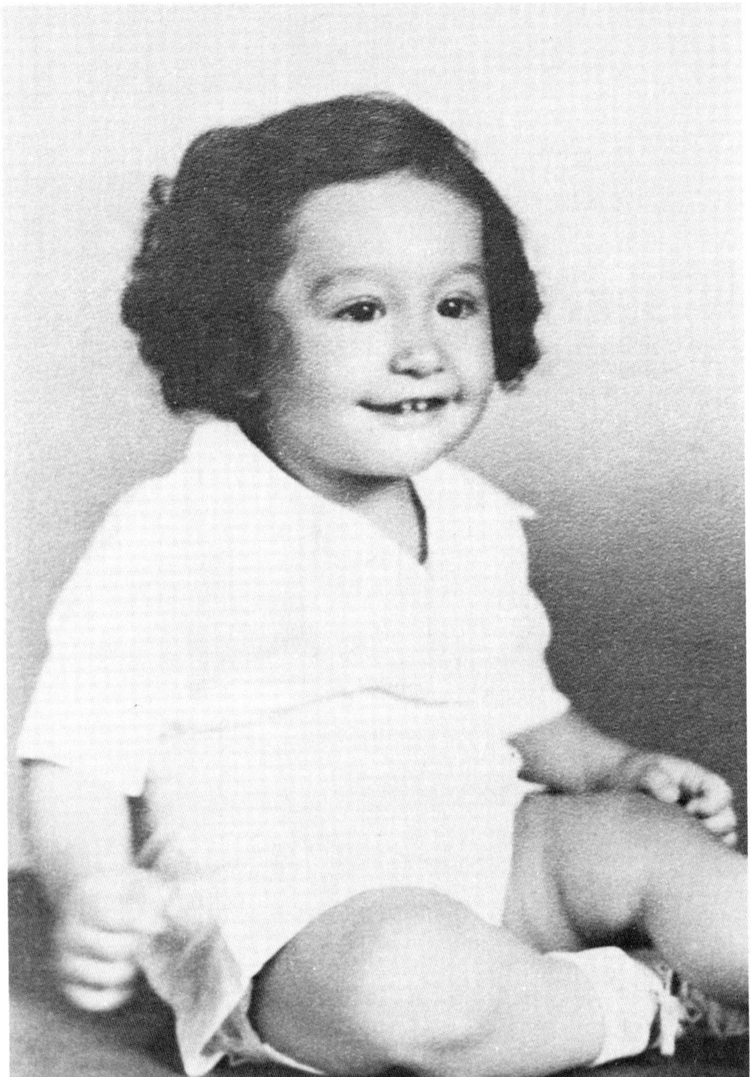

One of the first photographs of Henry.

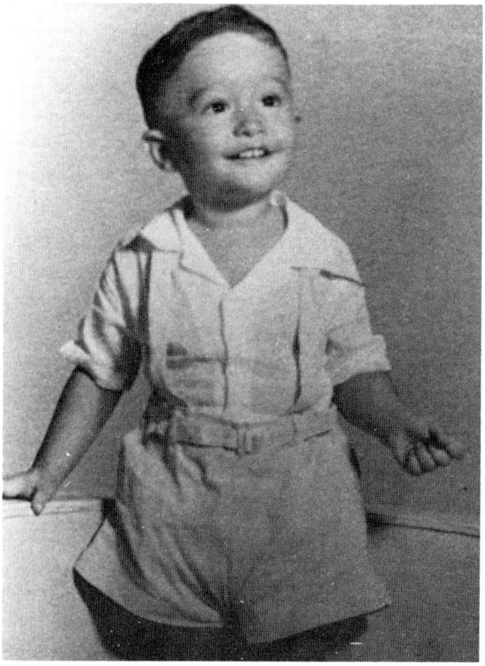

Henry was eleven months old when he had his first haircut.

shared meals, and, as devout Roman Catholics, went to mass every Sunday together.

The Cisneros house was a magnet for the neighborhood, especially in the summertime when school was out. Sometimes Henry's friends would come over as early as eight o'clock in the morning and stay until supper. If the Cisneros children were lucky, they could persuade some of their friends to help them with the chores, which included mowing the lawn, hosing down the patio, washing windows, and cleaning up their rooms. They once painted the garage to surprise Mr. Cisneros when he came back from a trip.

Between his family and his friends, Henry never had trouble getting activities and games going in the neighborhood. A whistle from someone's porch would bring out sixteen eager ballplayers as if by magic. Henry's best friend was a boy named Jesse Robledo; one day they cut their fingers, signed their names in blood, and became "blood brothers."

Henry calls his neighborhood a "Norman Rockwell kind of place." (Rockwell painted scenes from rural and small-town America that showed everyday people in daily routines.) He says that children belonged either to the Boy Scouts or the Girl Scouts. People had block parties and picnics, and shopped for groceries in small "mom-and-pop" stores. The barber knew everyone by name, and the doctors made house calls. "It was Norman Rockwell," Henry says, "but all the faces were brown."

The children spent hours running around the streets of the West Side, but time at home was also very important to them. Henry's mother encouraged her children to use their time creatively. Often Henry would spend his afternoon working on his airplane models. He loved airplanes, and liked to watch them flying overhead. Henry was a Little Leaguer, and one day when he was watching a jet—

Henry, five, and his sister Pauline, four, perform at a dance recital.

instead of the approaching fly ball—the ball hit him squarely in the face, breaking his nose.

When Henry wasn't building models, he was inventing many games and projects for his younger brothers and sisters. He would shout, "Let's build a ship!" and his "crew" would gather boards, rocks, and garden hoses to build a "ship." Henry also liked to write plays for his family to act in. At one point, someone decided that Pauline should be "Miss America," and the children spent the whole afternoon fixing up a dress, making a crown, supervising the contest, and, finally, conducting the coronation.

Though the children had fun together, misunderstandings and arguments would sometimes spring up between them. If any of the children misbehaved, the switch was never far away, but generally there was little need for it. "They were good children," Mrs. Cisneros said. "I can't complain."

Discipline was important to Henry's parents, and in many ways, the Cisneroses were a no-nonsense family. For Henry and his brothers and sisters, homework and chores always came before games or television. The family television was always turned off after "Disney World" on Sunday afternoons, and not turned on again until Friday

In the Little League, ten-year-old Henry played both as a pitcher and an outfielder.

evening; five days with no television gave the children plenty of time for studying at home and at the library. One summer, before entering the fifth grade, Henry read forty-three books!

Music played an important part in the Cisneros home. All of the family members liked to sing, and Henry, Tina, and Mrs. Cisneros all played the piano. Henry also played the French horn, and his brothers and sisters liked percussion instruments and the trumpet.

The Cisneros family enjoyed sharing meals together. Supper always began promptly at 5:30 P.M., and the conversations and laughter could last late into the evening. Henry's father would usually begin by relating something he had heard at work that day, or he would give details about a trip he was about to make. The children took many trips with their father; since he was in the military, he traveled to many seminars and training events all over the United States. No topic or question was off limits around the supper table, and the children would pick up their father's cues for discussion. "Do you know what happened in school today?" "Let me tell you what I read in a magazine!" Suppertime became an education in itself for the Cisneros children.

The family didn't always stay at home for their

The Cisneros family (left to right): *Pauline; Mrs. Elvira Cisneros; George, Jr.; Tina; George Cisneros; Henry; and Tim.*

meals; sometimes after a hard day's work at school or at home, they would pack up and go to a lake for a swim and a picnic, which often included a hot dog roast. "Report Card Night" also meant a special meal, regardless of what the grades were. For birthday celebrations, the children could choose any restaurant they wanted to go to, because their parents felt the experience of "eating out" and practicing good manners in a public place was very important. George and Elvira Cisneros also took their children to concerts, recitals, and an occasional movie.

Sunday afternoons were a special treat for the family. After church, they would sometimes go to the zoo, the stockyards, or visit the Missouri Pacific Railroad Station to watch the trains come and go. Most often, they would visit their grandparents, the Munguias, and hear exciting stories about Old Mexico. Young Henry came to care deeply about his Mexican heritage.

Grandfather Rómulo Munguia, Elvira's father, was born in Mexico, arrested while fighting for political freedom, and fled to the United States when his life and the lives of his family were threatened. He reached Texas in 1926, alone and without money. Finding a job as a journalist at a Spanish-language newspaper in San Antonio, he was soon able to bring his family to his new home. He saved his money until he could establish the Munguia Press, a print shop that continues to operate in San Antonio, managed by his son Reuben.

Henry spent hours with his Uncle Reuben at the print shop, sometimes doing odd jobs, but mostly listening to the Mexican refugees arguing about Mexican politics. His uncle told stories about all-night journeys to the Mexican border, either to pick up political refugees or to deliver others who were returning to Mexico to carry on their fight for equality and freedom.

Henry was proud of his family; his relatives were hard-working people who believed in freedom and democracy, as well as in education and self-discipline. Over the years, Henry would learn to apply these values to his own life.

Chapter Two

All-American Boy

Henry Cisneros did not speak very much English until he began kindergarten because Spanish was the language of San Antonio's West Side, and of course, of his family. When Henry was five years old, his parents decided to send him to the Little Flower School, which was a forward-looking, private elementary school run by the Roman Catholic church. Little Flower had excellent teachers and facilities for children of all racial and ethnic backgrounds, and Henry felt lucky to have Sister Mary Luke (now Sister Josephine McGarry) as his third-grade teacher.

Henry was among five of the third graders who caught the teacher's special attention. Because Henry seemed to be far ahead of many of the other

Little Flower School, that Henry attended through the eighth grade.

children in her class, and showed special leadership qualities, Sister Mary Luke allowed him to tutor the slower learners. In class, the teacher emphasized cooperation, interest, and the involvement of both the students and their parents. She also encouraged discussion and debate, because she wanted her students to learn to express themselves clearly. Class discussions established the facts, but they also built Henry's confidence in himself and his abilities.

Right after lunch, Sister Mary Luke would read stories, poems, and articles to her class. Taking an ordinary pencil, she would have the students analyze it. Where does a pencil come from? What is

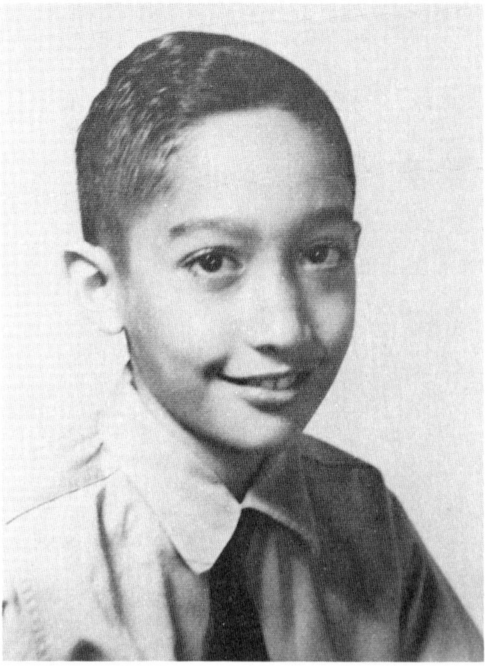

Henry in fifth grade.

natural in a pencil, and what is manufactured? The students enjoyed this method of learning about science and social studies.

Sister Mary Luke remembers Henry Cisneros well. She describes him as being rather shy, but she calls it a "nice shyness."

"He saw that certain things needed to be done, and he did them—but in an unassuming [modest] way," she recalls. "I know the term 'all-American boy' is overworked, but I think it really describes Henry when I knew him in the third grade. He studied hard and he played hard."

When each member of the third grade class

was given an achievement test, Henry and his four friends scored the highest. Sister Mary Luke decided to talk to the principal about allowing these five children to skip a grade. Henry did skip the fourth grade, but there was a price to pay. He had to go to summer school in order to complete the required fourth-grade subjects, which meant a lot of work for a young boy who would have preferred to play during the summer. Skipping a grade also made Henry a year younger than his classmates, though he had no problem competing with the older students.

Henry entered Central Catholic High School when he was only thirteen years old. Central had eight hundred students, all boys, and Providence High School, for girls, was just across the street. Although five hundred boys had competed for entry to the school, only two hundred were accepted.

By his sophomore year, Henry was on the cross-country team, playing the French horn in the band, and doing well in his studies. That year, Henry's mother learned that Brother Martin "Mac" McMurtrey (all the teachers were "Brothers" of a religious order) was offering an advanced English course, and went to the school to talk to him.

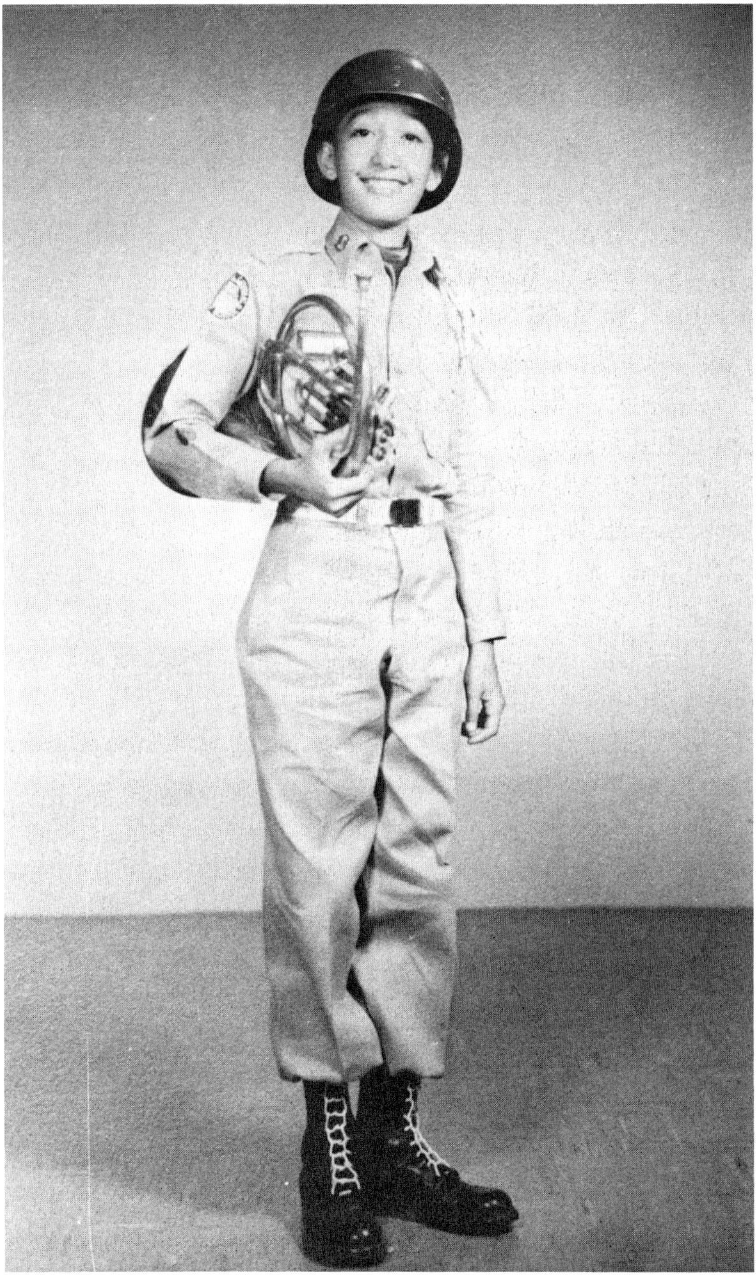

Henry poses with his French horn.

"Is Henry in advanced English?" she asked.

Brother Mac chuckles when he tells the story today. "Henry wasn't in the class, but I saw his mother was a determined lady and I didn't want a fight. So I decided then and there that Henry would be in advanced English!"

After a conversation with the registrar, the change was made. Henry's grades dropped slightly, but the advanced classes prepared him well for his continuing education. When he was a senior and took the SAT, a test for people wanting to attend college, Henry and everyone else in Brother Mac's class scored 99 percent in either English usage or vocabulary.

Brother Mac encouraged his students to work for these spectacular results. As a poet and a novelist, he knew and loved the English language. Not only did he drill the boys in grammar, he also inspired them (and required them) to write. Brother Mac edited an annual *Anthology* in which the best writing of his students was published.

Under Brother Mac, Henry also studied poetry and speech, and quickly learned how to think and speak on his feet. Five student names and speech topics were pulled from a hat, and each student had to speak intelligently about the chosen subject for seven full minutes. Ideas expressed through lan-

Brother "Mac" McMurtrey stands in front of Central Catholic High School.

guage held a special appeal for Henry. Brother Mac believes that Henry is a gifted speaker, and that his "genius" is "the spoken word and his ability to sway people with it."

One day in particular stands out in Henry's memory of high school: November 21, 1963. It was an unusually warm November day, and classes at Central Catholic High School were let out so that the students could walk to nearby Broadway Street and watch the motorcade of President John F. Kennedy and his wife, Jacqueline Kennedy. San Antonians poured out to see the president. Both President John Kennedy and his brother, Attorney General

Robert Kennedy, were especially popular among Mexican-Americans because, like themselves, they were both Democrats and Roman Catholics. In fact, in many homes, photographs of both Kennedys surrounded a picture of Our Lady of Guadalupe, the patron saint of Mexico.

The day after the motorcade went through San Antonio, the presidential party went to Dallas. There, President John F. Kennedy was assassinated. Henry was deeply moved by the president's death. Sixteen and now a senior, he wrote the following poem:

My Day Was Sunny

Happy children in the schoolyard play.
Autumn leaves, tainted golden honey,
Fall to earth, warm and gray,
My day is sunny.

Christ spirit already entraces the city.
Browns, yellows, and golds of autumn are a sight
To make wanderers look home wistfully.
My day is bright.

Even helpless creatures realize
That today there is little they need fear,
For on a day of such innocence none can despise.
My day is clear.

Workers bear their labors unconcerned.
Housewives open their windows. Magnificent!
This is the day the poets yearned.
My day is brilliant.

"Good morning," say people, and mean it.
Leaves, trees, earth—all are crimson, copper,
    bronze and scarlet
Like a flame from a golden torch forever lit.
My day is lucent.

Today is the epitome of life.
Today is love.
Today is chipped heaven.
My day is refulgent.

Breaking from Dallas, comes the bitter word,
That turns sunny day mournful black.
O day of delightful unreality! O day absurd!
A shot rang out. Our President is dead!

The sky is gloomed with overcast.
People stumbling along the streets cast eerie
    shadows.
Through the murky, obscure dusk the flag lowers
    to half-mast.
Day is dark.

Having his poem published in Brother Mac's *Anthology* meant a great deal to Henry, but at this stage of his life he had no intention of becoming a serious writer. Henry was interested in flying, and since four major air force bases were located in and around San Antonio, he had ample opportunity to watch new types of aircraft flying overhead. He wasn't making model airplanes anymore; now he wanted to fly those planes.

Henry was also interested in a girl named Mary Alice Perez, and his thoughts often wandered across the street from Central Catholic High School to Providence High School. He had first met her at his friend Jesse Robledo's birthday party when he was twelve and she was ten, but Mary Alice remembers first noticing Henry when she was modeling in a school fashion show. It wasn't exactly love at first sight—her impression of him then was that he was skinny and had big ears.

They continued to see each other casually at school and at church, because they lived in the same neighborhood. Although their parents were strict, and formal dating wasn't allowed, Henry invited Mary Alice on a first "official" date to a band party during his senior year and later asked her to the senior prom. It seemed that Henry was in love.

Henry was growing up, and it was time for him to start thinking about what he would do after high school. He knew he wanted to become a flyer, so he applied to the Air Force Academy in Colorado.

They turned him down because he was only sixteen years old, suggesting that he try again when he was a bit older. Henry's second choice was to go to Texas A&M University where he could become an army officer like his father. Henry was ready to take on the world.

Chapter Three

A Hands-on Guy

When Henry Cisneros arrived on the campus of Texas A&M in 1964, he was overwhelmed by the huge size of the campus, and by the school's many opportunities. Texas A&M is located in College Station, about 90 miles (144 kilometers) northwest of Houston. When it was founded in 1876 the "A&M" stood for "Agricultural and Mechanical." At one time, Texas A&M was a strict military school, famous for its football and farm programs, and its students were called "Aggies," a term based on the word agriculture.

Although Henry wasn't sure what he wanted to study at A&M, he knew he wanted to follow his father into a military career. He thought about becoming a paratrooper (a trooper who parachutes

The "Texas Aggie."

out of airplanes), a pilot, and a military medical doctor.

One of the first things Henry did on campus was join the Corps of Cadets, which was almost like joining the army. This group was part of the ROTC (Reserve Officer Training Corps) program, and at Texas A&M, it meant discipline. The cadets had their hair cut in a regulation flat-top, and wore uniforms which included riding breeches and polished leather boots. Henry enjoyed the "spit-and-polish" military atmosphere of the campus.

The time came for Henry to decide what he was going to major in. After considering his many possibilities, his love of language, and perhaps the influence of Brother Mac's high school classes, led him to major in English. Since he had also decided to be a paratrooper, he minored in military science.

At A&M, Henry was fortunate to receive special attention from J. Wayne Stark, a dedicated educator who was the head of the Memorial Student Center. Stark acted as an academic "talent scout," and over the years he has inspired dozens of A&M students to work hard and do their best at the university.

Stark discovered Henry Cisneros during Henry's sophomore year, and liked what he saw: an eager, pleasant Mexican-American with a sparkle in his eyes. Henry had already been chosen as the outstanding first-year cadet in his unit, and he was clearly a high achiever. Henry had, however, failed a course in calculus. Since it was his first time to fail a class, Henry wasn't too concerned about it, but he did have to repeat the course. Stark talked with some of Henry's professors about the calculus problem, and as he tells it, he "fussed a bit" with Henry.

He told the young student that he could be doing a lot more on campus if only he would work on improving his grades. Good grades, he said, would be essential to a future in the military, as well as for graduate schools. The most persuasive point in Stark's lecture was telling Henry that he wouldn't be able to participate in any extracurricular activies (such as the band), if he didn't get to work on his studies.

Henry then buckled down. "I was plumb surprised at the way he turned around," Stark said. Again Henry was named outstanding cadet in his unit, and by the end of his sophomore year he was selected to be the sergeant major of the three-hundred member Texas Aggie band, the highest post any junior could hold in that organization.

After completing his first two years at A&M, Henry received word that he had been accepted by the Air Force Academy, his first choice of schools when he was still a senior in high school. He decided to stay at Texas A&M. "I knew that not only was I going to survive," he said, "but I was going to perform in a competitive way." Henry observes that, "If you could handle yourself in the classroom, if your military performance was up to speed, if you had the leadership capabilities, then there was no limit to what you could do at A&M."

It took courage, though, for a Hispanic to be at A&M at the time Henry was there. Hispanics were a minority group at the university, and Henry often had to deal with racial prejudice. "The worst place I could have selected to go to college as a Hispanic in the sixties was A&M," he remembers. "Sometimes I got angry, but I had friends who went to other schools who came away worse than angry—having been put in their place. At A&M there is no place for you except the one you make for yourself."

Henry's father had once told him to "Play by the rules, and beat them at their own game," and Henry followed his advice. He kept getting A's, yet found time to play intramural football and basketball. Henry joined the "100-Mile-Club," a group of joggers who ran on the university's golf course and pledged to run at least 100 miles (160 kilometers)

Henry as a Texas A&M Cadet.

every semester. During his senior year, Henry was named commander of the Aggie band, the highest honor of the Corps of Cadets.

In addition to these activities, Henry held posts in four different Memorial Student Center organizations that planned, organized, and found funding for a wide range of university projects. At eighteen years of age, Henry Cisneros found himself in Houston or Dallas, talking to A&M alumni who had become executives in oil companies and banks. Stark says that Henry was a superb fund-raiser, and learned a lot about his abilities and how to work with people in every walk of life.

When a student journalist once asked Henry how he managed to do so much, he replied, "I just get things done that have to be done every day. I set aside a certain amount of time for studying, and then work around it!"

When he was twenty and a junior at A&M, Henry's classmates chose him to take part in the Conference on United States Affairs, held at West Point, the U.S. Army's military academy. Top student leaders came from all over the country to discuss and debate national and international issues.

At the time of this 1966 conference, the war in Vietnam was expanding. The United States had

Commander Cisneros of the combined Aggie bands at Texas A&M.

bombed North Vietnam and Cambodia, and the number of U.S. troops in Southeast Asia had approached the 400,000 mark. Americans hotly debated the war, while the fight for equality of blacks and whites raged throughout the United States. In 1966, race riots broke out in Chicago, Brooklyn, Cleveland, and Los Angeles.

During the West Point conference, Henry learned that American cities were in serious trouble. Overwhelmed by the knowledge of the other student leaders, Henry remained silent. He listened intently, though, as he thought of his own city of San Antonio.

On his flight back to Texas, Henry read that week's issue of *Time* magazine. The cover story was about Daniel Patrick Moynihan (now a senator from New York) who had just completed a study on the problems in cities across America. Something clicked for Henry. He realized that the survival of cities was important to him personally.

At Texas A&M he had been preparing himself for a military career, largely because his father had emphasized service to country over personal success. As Henry thought over what he had learned on his trip, he decided that "service to country" was not limited to the defense of one's country; it could also mean building the country and helping to improve the lives of its people. To Henry, this kind of public service seemed just as honorable as being a loyal soldier.

Back at Texas A&M, Henry became interested in the new field of study called urban planning, a field that examined city growth and changes, with an eye for what would "promote the general welfare of the people, with the greatest efficiency and economy." Henry decided to continue on at A&M to earn a master's degree in urban planning. As part of this advanced study program, he earned a student internship under San Antonio's city manager, Jerry Hinckel, as well as the job of assistant city manager of Bryan, Texas. (Later that year, in 1968, Henry was commissioned a second lieutenant and a distinguished military graduate.)

Meanwhile, Henry and Mary Alice were still seeing each other. Mary Alice was living in San Antonio, taking courses at San Antonio College and working in the international department of a local bank. The eight-hour round-trip drive between College Station and San Antonio was a difficult commute, but Henry usually found a way to get back to San Antonio once a month. Mary Alice, accompanied by members of the family, sometimes visited College Station. Henry was proud to show her off at A&M, especially at the football games.

In the second year of his master's program, Henry was given the opportunity to work on a year-long project. He chose the Model Cities program which was begun by President Lyndon Johnson, and based on the president's vision of a "Great Society" that would give special emphasis to cities and their problems. To Henry, the project seemed ideally matched to his studies and interest in urban planning.

Henry was lucky; of the eight programs available in Texas, he was selected to return to his own city of San Antonio. Not only that, but the Model Cities office was located right in the West Side neighborhood where Henry had grown up—across the street from his grandfather's print shop. Henry would serve as an assistant to Roy Montez, the director of the Model Cities program, from January 1969 to January 1970.

During this time, Henry listened to the complaints of the West Side residents who wanted repaved streets, libraries, and better sewers. As Henry says, "I learned during those years that the government is wise to put its money in physical projects—drainage projects, schools, swimming pools—because only physical projects leave a lasting legacy."

As part of the program, Henry would communicate the concerns of the community to the

A mariachi band plays at the wedding party of Henry and Mary Alice Cisneros. The family (left to right) *includes: Mrs. Cisneros (Henry's mother); Mrs. Perez (Mary Alice's mother); Henry; Mary Alice; and Henry's grandparents, Mr. and Mrs. Rómulo Munguia.*

conservative San Antonio city council members. The council resented the Model Cities program, so Henry had quite a job to perform. Henry learned much about citizen participation and the mechanics of making government work. "I'm a hands-on guy," he says. "I have to be in a situation, feel it, smell it, before I can understand it."

Meanwhile, Henry and Mary Alice were married in St. Agnes Catholic Church in San Antonio on June 1, 1969—eleven days before Henry's twenty-second birthday. Mary Alice was twenty. They had planned to marry during Henry's senior year at A&M, but postponed the wedding until he had entered his master's degree program.

After the wedding, Henry and Mary Alice moved into a small garage apartment on Magnolia Avenue. Though they both kept very busy with their jobs, they still made time to spend with friends and family. On weekends, they sometimes went on camping trips, or to outdoor barbecues at Henry's parents' house.

Henry received his master's degree in urban and regional planning in 1970. Henry's year in San Antonio with the Model Cities program convinced him that helping people in the cities was definitely the arena where he wanted to spend his life. But first, he felt he still needed more education, especially in finance and administration. To acquire those skills, he decided to go back to school, this time in the East.

Chapter Four

Henry C. to D.C.

In January 1970, Henry and Mary Alice Cisneros packed their belongings into an old Volkswagen convertible and journeyed to Washington, D.C. Henry had been accepted by George Washington University to study public administration, public finance, and statistics, and would be working toward a doctoral degree, or Ph.D. Neither Henry nor Mary Alice had any idea how they would pay for Henry's education, or even their living expenses in the nation's capital, but Henry believed in taking advantage of every opportunity to advance.

On his last day of work in the Model Cities program, Henry's fellow workers threw a party, and ordered a cake baked in the shape of the White House with letters on the icing that read: "Henry C.

to D.C.!" Many friends teased Henry about "taking over Washington," some even suggesting that he would run for president.

When Henry and Mary Alice arrived in Washington, they were in for some big disappointments. The weather that January was miserably cold, and housing proved to be very expensive. They had to stay with friends until they found a one-room apartment they could afford. Mary Alice was unhappy—she missed her parents and friends in San Antonio. She also discovered that she was pregnant.

By that time, Mary Alice had decided to look for a job in order to help with expenses, and finally found one in the international department of Riggs National Bank, translating Spanish to English. Since Henry and Mary Alice didn't have much money to spend, they entertained themselves by visiting friends, going on picnics, touring the free monuments and museums in the nation's capital, and watching an occasional movie.

Henry began school at George Washington University, but he also wanted to get some practical "hands-on" experience in urban management. Mary Alice thought that finding this kind of arrangement might be impossible, but Henry had been studying the job market in Washington, and felt fairly confident that he could work something out.

His first stop was to visit the office of the National League of Cities and Allen Pritchard, the associate director, whom he had met several months before at a Model Cities conference. Pritchard told Cisneros that the League wasn't employing student interns at that time, but he asked Henry to come in for an interview that Friday.

Pritchard and the other staff members were impressed with Henry. They couldn't offer Cisneros a part-time job, but Pritchard wanted to hire Henry as a full-time assistant. At first Pritchard was worried that Cisneros might not be able to handle a full load of studies at the university, and work full-time for him. Henry, however, welcomed the opportunity and, without hesitation, took on the job. As he worked at the National League of Cities office, Henry became familiar with the work and style of many different mayors.

Though handling two full-time responsibilities was rough, Henry had learned to handle a busy schedule from his fifteen-hour workdays at Texas A&M and in San Antonio, and working on the Model Cities project. Mary Alice became used to Henry's long hours from the earliest days of their marriage; "I learned to be independent enough to keep busy myself so that I wouldn't be just waiting for him to come home all the time," she says.

Henry was attending a National League of Cities convention in Florida when the Cisneros's first daughter, Teresa Angelica, was born two weeks ahead of the doctor's prediction. Fortunately, Henry's brother George, Jr. was there to drive Mary Alice over icy streets to the hospital, and Henry rushed back from Florida to be with his wife and his new daughter.

In 1971, at age twenty-three, Henry decided to apply for the White House Fellows program, in which fifteen to twenty people are selected from about three thousand applicants to work as assistants to White House staff or cabinet members. Henry was sure that he wouldn't have a chance against all of the highly qualified candidates but, despite his doubts, he was one of the sixteen winners of the 1971 fellowships. Pleased with his new opportunity, Henry resigned his position at the National League of Cities, and continued his doctoral studies at George Washington University.

White House Fellows were encouraged to interview for various White House positions. At the time of Henry's fellowship, President Richard Nixon was in office. Henry wanted to work for Vice-President Spiro Agnew but was instead assigned to

President Richard Nixon greets Henry Cisneros upon his appointment as a White House Fellow.

the office of Elliot Richardson, then the Secretary of the Department of Health, Education, and Welfare (HEW).

Although it was exciting for Henry to work with top government officials, he had his share of hard work. He had to do many routine jobs, sometimes called "go-fer" tasks—"go for this, go for that." In addition, Henry had to research plans for future HEW projects, and write memos, press releases, and even an occasional speech for Richardson. Cisneros attended many high-level staff meetings and wrote reports on congressional hearings.

He was sent on month-long trips to Southeast Asia and to Africa, where he could put to the test his ideas about city growth, and how government should respond to the needs of the people.

Henry often thinks about those trips. "In Africa, we visited Malawi, Zaire, and Zambia. In Asia, we visited Korea, Japan, Hong Kong, Singapore, and Thailand. I learned a lot about. . .the system that holds things together, like highways and irrigation. We go to the store and buy a loaf of bread, but do we know where it comes from, really? We turn on the faucet and get water. We are dependent upon things and people we can't see. In those undeveloped and developing countries I saw how the pieces fit together. . . .One leads to another. One depends upon the other."

Henry found a good advisor and friend in Richardson. The Richardsons often invited Henry and Mary Alice to concerts or the theater. When asked by reporters why he took time to help Cisneros, Richardson said, "Henry was then and he still is an extremely attractive human being. I wasn't only impressed by his grasp of policy issues. I was attracted to his genuineness." At another time Richardson called Henry Cisneros a "national asset."

Richardson and Cisneros often discussed politics, and Henry learned that survival in politics came not from scheming to find some better position, but doing the very best he could in the job he was in. Richardson also believed that to be successful in politics Cisneros would have to have people who would support him, vote for him, and stand by him, and counseled his young assistant to cultivate his political base in San Antonio.

He also felt Henry would benefit from some additional education, and he recommended Harvard University, near Boston, Massachusetts. Henry was still working toward his Ph.D. in public administration at George Washington University, but his course work was almost complete. All that was left for him to do was to complete a dissertation, an original book-sized study, about "The City Governmental Role in Economic Development."

Henry and Mary Alice thought about Richardson's suggestion for a long time. Mary Alice wasn't too happy with the idea of another move, because she enjoyed her job in the bank, and they were now living in a somewhat larger apartment on Sixteenth Street. Henry, however, felt that the idea to go to Harvard was a good one and, after all, his year as a White House Fellow was coming to a close. They decided to give Boston a try. Knowing that he could not afford to go to Harvard on his own, Henry applied to the Ford Foundation for financial aid.

His request was approved, and he was promised a grant of ten thousand dollars.

The first year in Boston was very hard on them. Henry and Mary Alice had to scrimp and save to make the ten thousand dollars last for two years. Mary Alice could not find a job, and they rented a basement apartment. Henry took courses in public administration at the John F. Kennedy School of Government at Harvard, in nearby Cambridge.

While studying in Boston, Cisneros was asked to teach at the Massachusetts Institute of Technology (MIT). Finally, he was earning some extra income for the family. During the time he was at MIT, he thought about pursuing another Ph.D. program there. He began some doctoral classes, but eventually decided that one Ph.D. would be sufficient.

The second year in Boston was much better for the young couple. Mary Alice found a job, a day care center for Teresa, and a nicer apartment, and, during that year, Mary Alice had the chance to visit her family in San Antonio. Henry was still in the military reserves (left over from his days at Texas A&M), and for three months he went to Fort Benning, Georgia, for training as an infantry officer. (He eventually completed training as an officer in the infantry and in heavy weapons, and was pro-

Henry as an officer in the U.S. Army Infantry, the largest arm of the Army. Infantrymen are trained to seize, occupy, and defend land areas.

moted to captain in the U.S. Army Reserves.)

Two years in Boston was enough; by this time, Mary Alice was weary of Henry's pursuit of education. He had a bachelor's and a master's degree from Texas A&M, a Ph.D. from George Washington University, and a master's degree from Harvard University. No wonder Mary Alice said, "It's time the student went out and found a job."

Henry was now twenty-seven years old. After finishing his dissertation, he was offered a faculty position in the Division of Environmental Studies at the University of Texas in San Antonio (UTSA). Happy at the prospect of heading home, the Cisneros family loaded up the old VW and began the 2000 mile (3200 kilometer) trek back to Texas. Mary Alice was happy to go back to San Antonio—she was pregnant again, and wanted to be "home" when her second child was born.

Although Henry looked forward to his new teaching position, as usual, another idea was growing. If he was going to spend his life helping people in the cities, he needed to follow Elliot Richardson's advice and begin to build a political base. He knew that a city election was coming up in San Antonio, and he thought about running for a seat on the council. He had many decisions to make on the long road trip back to Texas.

Chapter Five

Going Back Home

When Henry and the family arrived back in San Antonio in 1974, they chose to live in the same neighborhood where Henry and Mary Alice had grown up. Wayne Stark, Henry's old friend from Texas A&M, saw them shortly after they had returned to Texas.

"Still driving that old VW, I see!" said Stark.

"We can't afford anything else," Henry replied with a chuckle. "Besides, maybe it will become a political symbol."

Back in his own territory, Cisneros was ready to take on his new teaching position, and San Antonio politics. San Antonio was in a state of political confusion. Candidates were not judged as "Democrats" or "Republicans," but on whether they were "conservative" or "liberal" in their politics. Traditionally, conservatives do not want the government to interfere with free enterprise, while liberals usually believe that the government should get involved in regulating business when people are hurt by the actions of corporations.

Conservatives had run the city of San Antonio for twenty years under the banner of the GGL, the Good Government League. The GGL was made up of mostly wealthy "Anglo," or white, business people who wanted to bring back "good government" and to improve city services. For two decades, the GGL had the support of San Antonians, but there were now people who thought it was time for a change. Many felt the city of San Antonio was growing without any controls and that many of its citizens were not getting their fair share of benefits. The Mexican-American community, too, was dissatisfied with the GGL, believing that Hispanics had been neglected or ignored for too long by the Anglo-dominated city council.

The GGL saw themselves slipping from power, and decided that two forms of action might make a difference—selecting a woman to run for mayor, and finding a Hispanic-American candidate to run for city council in 1975. Henry's uncle, Reuben Munguia, suggested to some of his GGL clients that they consider his nephew Henry for the city council seat. Many on the council liked this well-educated and popular Mexican-American, but others had questions and criticisms. They wondered, for example, whether a Mexican-American Roman Catholic would take orders from the local Catholic archbishop instead of city officials.

Henry recognized this as a narrow-minded, prejudiced view of himself and his Hispanic background, and made it clear that he regarded politics and religion as two separate issues. Despite people's concerns, Cisneros was chosen to be one of eight GGL candidates for city council.

Though Henry Cisneros was confident that he would win, not everyone was so certain. Many of his Hispanic friends thought he had turned against his own neighbors. They couldn't understand why Cisneros would run on the GGL ticket that had represented the conservative business people for so long, instead of a more liberal group that would give more government support to Hispanics and other minority groups.

Even though Cisneros knew that the GGL did not have a history of responding to the needs of the Mexican-American community, he decided to identify himself with the Good Government League. He was not betraying the Hispanics; he believed that reforms in the city had to involve and benefit everyone, not just one group. Cisneros assured the people that he would vote as his conscience and research instructed him, not necessarily how the GGL wanted him to vote on any particular issue.

Cisneros conducted a whirlwind campaign. He held block parties and barbecues. His physical training as a jogger (he runs at least three times a week) gave him the stamina to walk the entire length of the city, talking to people as he went. He didn't have much money for mass media advertising, so he promoted himself everywhere he could, issued daily press releases, and also managed to be mentioned on most of the newspapers' front pages and interviewed on the evening television newscasts.

The Good Government League had sponsored nine candidates, but only three of them won. Henry Cisneros, twenty-seven years of age, became the youngest council member in San Antonio's history. Cisneros did not win because of a Mexican-American voter majority—they gave him a cautious 44 percent of their vote. The GGL accomplished their other goal in this election when Lila Cockrell became the first woman mayor of a major U.S. city.

This year had many happy moments for Cisneros. Just one month after the election, his second

Henry Cisneros puts on some comfortable shoes in preparation for a walk for the March of Dimes.

daughter, Mercedes Christina, was born. He was glad to be close at hand on the special day, but he was soon back to business with his new duties and responsibilities.

From the very beginning of his term on the city council, Cisneros was faced with problems—all related to the rapid growth of this South Texas city. The population of San Antonio was one million and still growing. As a city's population expands, its basic facilities, such as water, electricity, natural gas lines, roads, and sewers, must also expand. Henry's education in urban planning helped him understand these problems, and how to treat them.

Henry Cisneros was determined to learn all he could about life in the city. He collected garbage with the garbage collectors, rode in police patrol cars, went to fires on the firetrucks, interviewed prisoners in jail, and visited nursing homes. Television newspeople saw these as interesting stories, so Cisneros got plenty of free publicity which kept him in the public eye even after the election.

Cisneros's main goal as a politician was to help the people of his city. He tried to avoid a political label, such as Democrat or Republican, because he wanted to consider the needs of all of San Antonio's groupings. Many people had difficulty guessing which way Cisneros would decide on a city

Henry Cisneros once worked as a garbage collector to learn more about how a city is run.

issue, because he didn't seem to "take sides." He formed a bridge between conservatives and liberals, which was often a no-win situation. Conservatives often criticized him for supporting government programs, and liberals accused him of being too "big business"-oriented.

One example of when Cisneros managed to anger both political groups was during the discussions of the city's water supply—a very important problem in the dry Southwest. At one point, a land developer requested permission from the city council to build a huge shopping mall over the Edwards Aquifer, a natural source of the city's drinking water. Acres of buildings and parking lots threatened the quality of water in the aquifer.

After much debate, the council voted to allow the mall to be built, but Cisneros fought their decision. He argued that if the aquifer became polluted, then the city would have to pay for equipment to clean the water. Cisneros supported the neighborhood and environmental groups who asked for a referendum, or citywide vote, on the matter. The people of San Antonio finally voted against building the mall.

The environmental groups were pleased with Cisneros's efforts, but the developers were angry. His next vote would surprise both groups. When the environmentalists wanted to call an eighteen-month moratorium, or delay, on *all* construction over the aquifer, Cisneros was opposed to it. Though many were shocked at his vote, he stood firmly, explaining that such a delay would be considered unconstitutional. The Edwards Aquifer issue was one of many that Henry Cisneros would grapple with as a city council member.

Cisneros worked long hours in city hall, as well as at the University of Texas in San Antonio. Mayor Lila Cockrell was always impressed with the number of books Henry read, and how he kept up with the problems of other American cities. Henry wasn't satisfied with just reviewing what others had done; he decided on his own plans and proposals.

When Cisneros again ran for city council in 1977, the voting procedures were different. The U.S. Justice Department had ruled, in 1976, that San Antonio's elections were not fair to such minorities as Mexican-Americans and blacks, because the addition of suburbs to the cities had brought in so many more white voters.

Cisneros campaigned strenuously for the charter amendment that would divide the city into equal districts and strengthen the voting powers of minorities. As a result of the election that followed, the city council was made up of five Mexican-Americans, one black, and five whites. For the first time in San Antonio's history, the "minorities" were the majority on the city council, six to five. Cisneros easily won his district and this time was re-elected by 92 percent of its voters. "I've learned the ropes now," he told them. "In the next two years I'm going to produce!"

But Cisneros was not always successful. He hoped to be named "mayor pro tem," a person who fills in for the mayor when the mayor is ill or traveling out of the city. Cisneros thought he had the votes and the support that he needed, including the support of Mayor Cockrell. When the council voted against him six to five, with Cockrell providing the sixth vote, he was hurt and angry.

Furious, Cisneros wrote a letter of resignation to the council. He didn't submit it formally to the mayor but he did tell a radio news reporter about it, who then broadcast his decision. Cisneros reconsidered his action during the night and the next morning informed a news conference that he had made a mistake, that he would not resign. "It's good to be taught a lesson," he said. "It's good to be humble."

Henry was also learning a lesson from his father, George Cisneros. In 1976, Mr. Cisneros had a stroke which paralyzed his left side. Although he

The Cisneros home in San Antonio, as it looked when Henry's grandfather lived there.

was forced to retire from the military, he was determined not to spend the rest of his life in a wheelchair. He learned to play golf and traveled to many new places. This display of courage and determination often gave Henry the strength he needed to move forward.

During his second term as city council member, Henry and Mary Alice bought their first home, the fifty-year-old house that Grandfather Munguia once owned. Located at the corner of Houston and Pinto streets, the house is about equal distance from Henry's parents and city hall.

In 1979, Cisneros again campaigned and was re-elected to a third term on the city council. During this term, most of the debates and arguments on the council were about money. How large a budget could taxpayers afford? What were the best, most useful ways to spend city money? There were ongoing disagreements about city growth, as well as important questions about the needs of minorities.

Politics has been defined as the "art of the possible." Henry Cisneros learned to listen, to understand the other side of a question, to decide, and to persuade other council members to change their minds. Henry was learning what was possible to achieve within a community composed of many different groups of people.

Henry has always believed deeply in democracy—people working together on problems for the benefit of all citizens. Becoming San Antonio's mayor would give him the chance to bring the city together and, in 1981, he decided that his time had come to run for election.

Henry Cisneros faced one major obstacle, however. The mayor at that time was Lila Cockrell, a friend of Henry's, and he didn't want to run against her if she were going to run again. Cisneros would not make any announcements until he knew that she would not be a candidate, but it was difficult for him to wait for her decision.

As it turned out, Cockrell decided not to run for a 1981 re-election. She enjoyed her job very much, but since her husband had suffered a mild heart attack earlier in the year, they both felt that they should devote more time to their personal lives. She is sure, even today, that Cisneros would have entered the race regardless of her decision.

Henry wasted no time when he heard the news. At the historic Menger Hotel, he announced that he would be an independent candidate for mayor, and requested supporters for his campaign. His opponent was John Steen, a successful insurance salesman, millionaire, and three-term member of the city council. Although neither candidate ran under a political party label, it was generally understood that Steen was a Republican and that Cisneros was a Democrat. (Actually, Cisneros wouldn't be officially considered a Democrat until 1983.)

During the 1981 campaign, many San Antonians were struck by Cisneros's winning personality, his incredible energy, and his hopeful visions for the future of the city. A very persuasive and enthusiastic speaker, he tried to convince the voters that they should unite behind his ideas, and that only he could bring San Antonio together. He emphasized the need to generate new business for the city, and the need for plenty of good water and inexpensive energy.

This campaign gave Henry the chance to show

On the front steps of San Antonio's city hall, Henry Cisneros clowns around with a crowd of children.

what he had learned about running for election in San Antonio. Since 1975, his first year on the city council, Cisneros had been keeping an indexed card file of the names of people he thought would support him. He now had names of more than 90,000 San Antonians in that file, and a team of seventy volunteers who would help organize his campaign, under the direction of his brother George, Jr. A rather surprising number of young real estate developers, union members, school teachers, and special interest groups such as Communities Organized for Public Service (COPS) agreed to support him.

By April 1981, there were six Cisneros campaign centers around the city, and a 24-hour-a-day operation in the city's center. About $250,000 was raised. San Antonians heard about Cisneros's views on the issues on radio and television; they also heard about the campaign in their homes, either by way of a personal visit or by telephone. On election day, volunteers used two hundred telephones to call at least 40,000 supporters, to remind them to vote.

The campaign captured national attention, and the media pegged Henry Cisneros as the symbol of a growing Hispanic population. The *New York Times*, *Time*, *Newsweek*, and even *La Prensa* from Mexico City sent writers to interview Cisneros. On

Henry and his family ride along in a parade in the well-recognized Volkswagen convertible, Henry's political symbol.

election day, April 4, 1981, the total number of voters reached 155,831—a new record turnout for San Antonio. Henry Cisneros was elected mayor, receiving 61.8 percent of the vote. His family was thrilled. Mary Alice, Teresa, and Mercedes rode with Henry in a victory parade in the old Volkswagen convertible. The car had become his political symbol, just as Henry had predicted.

Chapter Six

Mister Mayor

Although being elected mayor of San Antonio meant a great responsibility and a lot of work for Henry Cisneros, it also was a source of pride for him and his family. He had dreamed of being mayor since his days at the National League of Cities office, and he was eager to get started on his new job.

Mayor Cisneros has accomplished much for San Antonio just by serving as its representative. Perhaps the best way to describe his duties is to say he is an active "salesperson" for his city, though he is also active in developing his own "product"—the city of San Antonio.

Cisneros has strong convictions about the growth of San Antonio. He believes that the city's

Mayor Henry Cisneros.

real problems can be solved not by getting more help from the state government, but by building up the city's economy. He hopes to accomplish this by bringing in more businesses and tourists, and creating more jobs and schools for the people of San Antonio.

Early in his first term as mayor, Cisneros had the chance to follow up on his ideas. The University of Texas in San Antonio was considering the idea of expanding its program to include a state-supported engineering school, but it seemed as though they were going to pass up the chance. For Cisneros, the engineering school meant hope for San Antonio's future economy, and along with other supporters, he fought hard for the school.

In front of the university's governing board at the state capitol in Austin, Cisneros spoke persuasively on the part of young San Antonians. He pointed out that many students were eager for an education, but that few could afford it if they had to leave the city to get it. His closing argument was that either San Antonio would produce engineers and other professionals to help out Texas, or the state of Texas would have to provide more welfare dollars to unemployed San Antonians.

When Cisneros finished speaking, the board applauded loudly, and the next day they voted to add the engineering school. The several hundred engineers who now graduate each year from this school are beginning to fill the needs of the increasing number of computer-based industries in the area.

The next project for the new mayor was to make San Antonio a part of the international trend toward an "information industry" based on communication and computer services. To express his views on the importance of technology to a city, he squeezed the time into his busy schedule to write the "orange book," or *San Antonio's Place in the Technology Economy.* His efforts were successful; more high-tech schools have been created in San Antonio, and Control Data, a major computer corporation, now has a base in the Alamo City. Cisneros has a dream of a high-tech computer corridor between San Antonio and Austin; a "teleport," a center for communications in the future; and a leading biomedical center in San Antonio. Some have criticized Cisneros for rushing the city into the future.

His positive outlook on the progress of San Antonio, however, was earning the confidence of the city's residents. Henry Cisneros was re-elected to a second term as mayor in 1983 by an amazing 94.2 percent of the vote. No previous candidate had ever received such a high number of votes, and that 1983 victory will never be forgotten in San Antonio.

Soon after his re-election, Mayor Cisneros announced a "Target 90" program which brought together more than five hundred San Antonians, from all sections of the city, to plan definite goals for the 1990s. The group, which included some city council members, worked for eighteen months and agreed on 170 goals for the city. The goals covered many possibilities, from completing the Austin-San Antonio high-tech corridor, to helping many of the city's adults learn to read and write.

Henry Cisneros's name was rapidly gaining national recognition. On July 19, 1983, he was chosen by President Ronald Reagan to be a member of the National Bipartisan Commission on Central America headed by former Secretary of State Henry Kissinger. This commission was designed to examine the affairs of El Salvador and Nicaragua in Central America. Cisneros was at first considered a "safe" member to have on the largely conservative commission, because many thought he agreed with Reagan's stand on foreign policy issues. Cisneros surprised the conservatives—he had serious questions and concerns about the U.S. involvement in Latin America, and felt obligated to act as a bal-

President Ronald Reagan greets Henry Cisneros upon his return from Central America.

ancing force on the committee. "It was a strange experience in a way," Cisneros said, "because the usual criticism against me is for being too much of a diplomat. . . .And here. . .I was perceived as the wild, flaming, uncontrollable bomb-throwing member of the group."

Although there were some tense moments on the commission, Cisneros managed to work out his differences with the other members of the committee. His views on foreign policy were not "wild" and radical; in fact, they were shared by many moderate Democrats, including Walter Mondale. Cisneros and Mondale developed a relationship that would once again put Henry in the public eye.

Henry Cisneros and his family join Walter and Joan Mondale on July 4, 1984. Henry attempts to describe jalapeño candy to the skeptical reporters.

In 1984, Cisneros entered the national spotlight when he was considered as a possible vice-presidential running mate for Democrat Walter Mondale. The whole Cisneros family went to Saint Paul, Minnesota, to visit Mondale before the interviews. At first, Mary Alice was against bringing Teresa and Mercedes because she thought the trip might put too much pressure on them. Henry wanted them to go, and promised them the best Fourth of July they ever had. Mary Alice brought along a basket filled with suckers shaped like bluebonnets (the Texas state flower), jalapeño pepper candy, and a sugar replica of the Alamo. Henry's daughters not only met the Mondales, but also saw many of the national television reporters. What the girls remember most of all, though, were the mosquitoes and bugs that bit their legs as they stood together in a press conference!

Cisneros was confident in himself. He told the reporters, "I believe that I could do the job [of vice-president]. I'm confident in my abilities and I really trust the basic instincts that I have honed over seventeen years of government work. Those don't add up to the traditional qualifications that we think of in terms of a vice-presidential selection, but at this point in our country's history, they are as important as traditional qualifications."

Though Cisneros did not become Mondale's running mate, the whole experience was a valuable one. He gained nationwide attention and a greater sense of his political potential.

In 1985, Cisneros joined the faculty of Trinity University as a visiting professor of urban studies. For most of his first two terms as mayor, Cisneros was not allowed to accept payments from the city because he was being paid by the University of Texas, another government-backed institution. Now he could earn a decent salary both from Trinity and the city, because Trinity is a privately owned school.

Being a professor became increasingly difficult with Cisneros's busy lifestyle. His schedule is tight, and he must frequently cancel many of his appointments. "I am a professor," he says, "and I think I'm a good teacher, and that my students learn a lot. But I don't enjoy teaching as much as I once did, mostly because I can't give teaching enough time. I don't have the time to do the research or write the books that professors are supposed to do. So when people ask me what I do for a living, I answer 'I'm a mayor.' I am happy to be a public servant."

Enjoying his life as a public servant of San Antonio, Cisneros decided to run for his third term as mayor in 1985. He worked hard to convince the people to believe in his ideas, and his own performance in politics. "People need to know what you've done," he says. "There are times when you won't want to do this—for reasons of propriety, sincerity, or modesty. But your competitors, who may not be as well-qualified as you, can beat you in a political contest just because they understand the importance of publicity."

A typical day of Cisneros's 1985 campaign began with a visit to the Black Baptist Ministers' Association. Then he rushed over to a luncheon meeting with the San Antonio Manufacturers' Association and, after lunch, huddled with military

The mayor urges the passage of certain bonds in his 1985 re-election campaign.

leaders at Fort Sam Houston. In the late afternoon, he held a press conference in northwest San Antonio.

Cisneros made the same presentation everywhere, but each time it was different. He adjusted what he wanted to say, depending on where he was, to whom he was speaking, and how much time he had to speak. This time, Cisneros didn't talk about himself or his past administration. Rather, he promoted ideas he felt were necessary to San Antonio's future: increased police protection, more traffic lights, improved freeway systems, restoration of run-down areas of the city, and the addition of more companies and industries to his city.

Everywhere Cisneros went, he knew people by name and often asked a personal question about a member of the family. A capable and wise politician, Cisneros was smooth and intelligent, but he also demonstrated an understanding of people and their interests. What's more, he seemed to sincerely enjoy campaigning.

And his 1985 campaign worked; Cisneros won his third term as mayor with 73 percent of San Antonio's vote. In 1987, he won again, with 67 percent of the vote. Since his re-election in 1987, Mayor Cisneros has continued to put his many ideas for his city into action.

Throughout his terms as mayor, Cisneros has actively tried to bring more and more visitors to San Antonio. Tourism is big business in the Alamo City. The historic Alamo attracts thousands of tourists to the city, as does the beautiful, wandering, miles-long River Walk. The HemisFair, San Antonio's World's Fair built in 1958, has also introduced many people to the city. San Antonio is home to both the San Antonio Symphony and the San Antonio Spurs, a professional basketball team. Another tourist attraction is La Villita, a replica of a colonial Mexican village.

Cisneros has fought to bring Sea World, a marine park, to San Antonio. The Sea World proj-

The historic Alamo.

ect would bring many sea creatures, two thousand new jobs, a thousand-room hotel, and a new research center to San Antonio. Cisneros also dreams of having a stadium built in San Antonio, because he firmly believes that a major city should be able to attract major sporting events. Cisneros did try hard to attract the Olympic Festival to the city, but was not successful. He is, however, negotiating with the NFL to bring a football team to the city, and major league baseball may also find a home, and fans, in San Antonio.

Some of Cisneros's critics say that the mayor's energetic pursuit of new tourist attractions has gone

Located in downtown San Antonio, the River Walk, or Paseo del Rio, offers a collection of shops, restaurants, hotels, and night clubs.

too far. People have said that the mayor should spend less time advertising the city, and more time tending to the city's real needs and problems. Cisneros is criticized for traveling too much and making too many speeches. Some San Antonio citizens say that he isn't all that interested in being a mayor, because he has his sights set on some higher political office.

If in some ways his ambition and his enthusiastic appeal for San Antonio have earned him criticism, they have also made Henry Cisneros and the city of San Antonio famous. During his terms as mayor he has been awarded many honors, awards, memberships, and honorary degrees for his political achievements. Cisneros was named one of America's ten outstanding young men in 1982 by the Jaycees (the Junior Chamber of Commerce) and has been featured on "Sixty Minutes." He is a member of many organizations, including the Texas Municipal League, and was elected president of the National League of Cities, where he had worked during college. Cisneros is a trustee of Notre Dame University, and has earned many honorary degrees from schools around the nation.

Chapter Seven

The Next Step

Henry Cisneros has often said that he is happy being a mayor. His friends and foes both feel that Cisneros has a great deal of potential—and that he will not end his political days in San Antonio's city hall. Some thought that Mayor Cisneros would become a candidate for governor of Texas in the election of 1990. When the popular Lieutenant Governor William Hobby took himself out of the 1990 governor's race, many saw this as a golden opportunity for Cisneros to become the first Mexican-American governor of Texas.

But Henry's plans have changed. One day before Henry's fortieth birthday, Mary Alice gave birth to a son, John Paul Anthony Cisneros. Born on June 10, 1987, he was twenty inches long, but

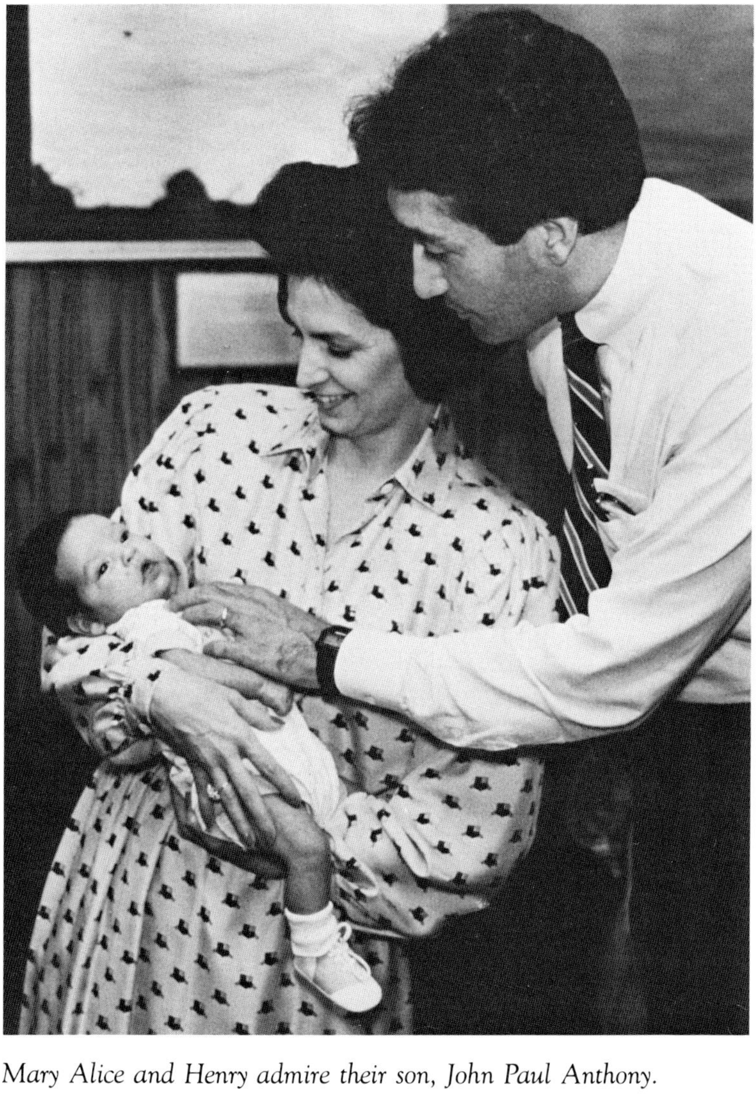

Mary Alice and Henry admire their son, John Paul Anthony.

The Cisneros home, with its new additions.

weighed only five pounds and fourteen ounces. The baby boy was born with a defective heart and without a spleen, an organ that monitors the blood. Since his health is uncertain, John Paul will require medical help and much loving care.

The baby was named in honor of Pope John Paul II, who visited San Antonio in 1987, and his middle name Anthony honors "San Antonio." Henry and Mary Alice are thrilled to have a son, and have added an extension with a third bedroom to their West Side home.

John Paul has deeply affected the political plans of his father. Henry has said officially that "the family stress associated with John Paul's care requires attention that is not compatible with gearing up for any major statewide effort.'' In other words, for the time being, Henry is putting his family ahead of any ambitions of higher elective office.

It hasn't been an easy decision, and Henry is under a great deal of pressure. Many people in the Democratic party feel that Cisneros should run for some higher office for the sake of the party, and some Hispanics say he has abandoned them and their cause. Despite the pressures from all sides, when John Paul was born, Henry declared his need for ''private family time.''

Family is very important to Henry. Even with his fifteen-hour-a-day schedule, he tries to spend as much time as he can with them. He also still keeps closely in contact with his brothers and sisters. Pauline is a biologist who works in Galveston, Texas. His brother George, a San Antonio resident, is a composer and musician, and his other brother, Tim, is an architect who has completed studies in Paris, France, and now lives in Dallas. Tina, Henry's youngest sister, has a degree in journalism, and lives in New Jersey.

Family life for Henry is different from his own childhood days with his brothers and sisters. There are fewer shared meals and table conversations—

The Cisneros family (left to right): *Mercedes, Mary Alice, Henry, and Teresa.*

Henry simply doesn't have as much time. There aren't the long trips Henry once used to enjoy, following the schedule of his army father. Henry does travel with his family whenever he can fit it into his work schedule. On a trip to Corpus Christi, where Henry was scheduled to give a speech, the family went along and enjoyed the weekend together. They swam, jogged, saw a movie, and enjoyed eating out in restaurants. The longest vacation they've ever had was four days on a borrowed boat. In order to spend more time with each other, the Cisneros family hopes to build a cabin on Lake LBJ in the Texas hill country. The birth and special needs of John Paul, though, have brought the Cisneros family closer than ever.

Henry looks forward to intelligent conversations with his daughters. He is proud of them, and feels that they show good judgment as they work at being informed about the world. Both Teresa and Mercedes are hard-working students and good musicians. They both love animals, and have had a cocker spaniel, a rabbit, and a cat. Henry was proud of Teresa when she was elected vice-president of her junior class and when she became a "candystriper," a volunteer who delivers mail and gifts to patients, at a nearby hospital. He was just as proud of Mercedes when she joined a cheerleading squad.

Teresa greets her father at the San Antonio International Airport. Her sister, Mercedes, waits her turn.

Henry admires his wife Mary Alice. Among her many other jobs, she has worked as the director of special projects and community relations for a large photo-processing plant, and has also volunteered for the Literary Council, Texans Against Hunger, and for other social agencies. Henry says of Mary Alice, "My wife and I grew up together, and she's always, frankly, gotten to me in a way that I really can't quite explain."

The family has had to adjust to the celebrity status of Henry. When they go out to dinner, it's the mayor who has to stand up, accept greetings, and sign autographs. There are a few public functions the family can't avoid, such as groundbreaking and ribbon-cutting ceremonies, and fundraising events. Being the wife and children of a politician has its requirements.

But it also has its rewards—the excitement of political life provides the opportunity to see new places and become acquainted with important public figures. The family is as proud of Henry as he is of his family.

Henry says that, for him, it is difficult to distinguish between public time and private time. As a "public servant" all of his time is "public time." Once he accepts that fact, he says, life is easier. "Once I was invited to a 'house blessing,' a tradi-

Henry participates in a ground-breaking ceremony for a neighborhood center.

tional Mexican-American event. In the old days it would have been a 'chore,' something for which I had to get ready. Almost as soon as I arrived I would count the minutes until I could break away, go home, relax. Now I just consider something like this part of my 'private time.' I enjoy the people who are there, the conversation, and the breeze under the patio. That's a different approach to life than the way I used to live. Now I try to find my solace, my enjoyment, and my reserves of strength in the event where I happen to be."

When he does manage to find time alone, Henry takes the opportunity to read. Although a couple of his office shelves are occupied by his model airplanes, Henry's office is lined with books. He reads an occasional novel but most of his reading includes biographies and books discussing politics. Two of his favorite biographies are William Manchester's *American Caesar* (about General Douglas MacArthur) and James M. Burns's *The Lion and the Fox* (about President Franklin D. Roosevelt).

Henry may eventually decide to remove himself from politics and the public eye. He has hinted that he might consider an offer from the business community; he has the qualifications to be the chief executive officer of any major corporation. Many major universities in the United States would be eager to have him as a professor, or even as a president.

However, it is possible that the excitement of government has crept into his blood to such a degree that nothing else will satisfy him. Without blinking an eye, he once told a reporter that he was capable of serving as president of the United States. For Cisneros, politics has become a way of life.

A vacancy in the Congress or a strong challenge to his ideals could encourage him to run for either the House of Representatives or the Senate. A future Democratic administration might nominate him for a cabinet post in Washington; many people think Cisneros would make an excellent secretary of either the Department of Housing and Urban Development or the Department of Commerce. He might again be considered good vice-presidential or even presidential timber; he might yet try for that Texas governorship. Or Cisneros may be satisfied to continue on as mayor of San Antonio.

Despite all the speculation about Cisneros's future, the mayor is convinced about the future of American cities. "The choice for cities isn't between going forward or standing still. You either go forward or you slide backward. It isn't a question of whether growth will occur, nor when. It is only a question of how we prepare for that growth and what we want to accomplish. And," Cisneros says with confidence, "that kind of growth can be managed."

Cisneros has pushed San Antonio forward in many areas. Concentrating on providing more jobs for San Antonians, he has sought to bring in new businesses. He has helped establish an engineering school to prepare students for high-tech jobs, and he has stimulated the city's tourist industry. As a representative of San Antonio, he has traveled all over the country to speak for his city.

His unique approach to politics, as well as his appeal to both Hispanics and Anglos, conservatives and liberals, Republicans and Democrats, have brought the different communities of San Antonio together in a way that no other mayor had achieved before. As many have said of Cisneros, he has been the "right Hispanic at the right time."

Cisneros has worked hard to bring his city into the national spotlight, and he has high hopes of developing San Antonio into something more than the Alamo City. More and more people are learning of the possibilities and opportunities in a growing San Antonio. Cisneros believes that "there is still much to be done," and with his tireless enthusiasm and energy, he may just see to it that much gets done—in and beyond San Antonio.

Chapter Eight

Some Words from Cisneros Himself

Henry Cisneros has a list of personal guidelines—forty-three of them to be exact. These make up a kind of personal road map that Cisneros has followed, both as a city planner and as mayor.

As a professor of urban planning and government at Trinity University in San Antonio, Cisneros communicates these principles in a speech called, "On Exercising Personal Influence in a Public Policy Setting."

Cisneros reviewed these guidelines, and rewrote them especially for this book. Of the forty-three, he selected twenty-four of the ones he felt would be the most helpful to young people who want to make the most of their educations and their future careers.

Henry Cisneros sits in his office, reviewing his chapter of this book.

Some Words I Live By

by Henry G. Cisneros

1. *When you seem to come to a standstill, look ahead and focus on the positive.*
If you're in a dark cave, find those cracks or slivers of daylight that will show you the way out. Find solutions in situations where there is a lot of heat and argument. Remove the fuse from that kind of explosive "bomb." In other words, where there are many people with many opinions, you can't make progress without finding that little sliver of daylight. I learned this from Lila Cockrell, when she was mayor. She constantly looked for something positive where there was only opposition. That's a very important attitude for a leader to have. Don't add to the confusion. Keep talking and try to smooth over the differences. Talking is always better than fighting.

2. *Know the difference between "getting things done" and "busy work."*
It's so easy to become trapped by routine. You can spend a whole day and say, "I'm really tired, I

worked hard today" but when you look at what was done, nothing really important was accomplished. It was just shuffling papers, and "pushing buttons." At the end of a day, I think it's important to ask myself "What have I done today that made the world a better place?"

3. *Learn the value of time.*

Learn that any lost time cannot be regained. It is a limited *resource,* just like water or oil. Everyone agrees with this idea but so few people, in my judgment, put the proper value on time.

4. *Keep your mind aware of unresolved problems.*

I have a kind of "antenna" that seems to remain slightly tingling as long as there is an ongoing problem that must be dealt with. That doesn't mean I'm always worried about a certain problem. It does mean I intend to deal with it. Somebody gives me some news and I quickly sift through it; is there a problem that's likely to arise down the road because of this piece of information? Perhaps there is an opportunity? I like to think of it as a catalog-drawer in the library where you leave a card slightly out of position. That's the card your eye always goes to. Your mind can work that same way, too. You don't have to solve everything right this minute—but there will be important problems and questions that you'll have to get back to.

5. *Learn to translate goals into action.* Goals are those things you want to accomplish in the future ("What do I want to achieve or happen three months from now, or a year from now?") Focus on action plans and next steps ("What do I want to do, or what do I want to happen today or next week?"). Check your progress against those longer-range goals.

6. *Always be prepared to be flexible.* Take your cue from a football quarterback. There are lots of different plays. There are changes you will have to make even after a play is called. Don't be flat-footed! Expect things to change—because life, throughout your life, is always changing. There may be changes for the worse, as well as for the better.

7. *Sometimes in order to make progress we must first work at not sliding back.* It is important to take time to prevent the worst of what might happen. You may be confronted with a bad situation and you say to yourself, "Well, that's certainly not moving ahead." But sometimes you've got to take time to deal with that bad situation just to "stay put." Be glad that you really saved time from having to correct the situation later. There are many times when it's necessary for me to call an emergency meeting to "put out a fire."

Mayor Cisneros answers a phone call in his office as he goes through some photographs for this book.

Example: right now I've got a call from a person in the police association. It's worth it to me to make time, to juggle my schedule, to see him and to help get that police association on a more positive track, than to risk the breakdown of the whole police department. It may not look like progress. But we're not sliding backward. And that's something positive.

8. *Hold to your personal vision of what you can do.* To expect gratitude—or thanks—in public service is the wrong reason for being in public service. Instead, be satisfied with things like your personal character, a sense of duty, and your own personal vision (or dream) for what you can do. If people appreciate you, fine. If not, just keep your vision—and press onward.

9. *Leave something that will last.* Keep a sense of balance. Admit that a person's public work is never finished, because the world never stands still. Thus your goals should focus on how you leave something that has "staying power." Teach people. Build institutions that will last. Plan methods or ways to help people, not handicap them.

Part of keeping your balance is to realize that there is always room for other people, for their ideas and for their work. They have contributions to make. Life does not revolve around one person. Life does not revolve just around you and me.

10. *Be careful of details.*

I stress this point with students. Lack of attention to the final 5 percent of the work will undo 95 percent of good work. I try to "walk through" problems and circumstances in my mind, *before* they occur. This prepares me for pressure situations. If you write a paper or make a speech, review every element so you get the details just right. Time and again I have seen good work undone by the missing element that wasn't more than 5 percent of the total effort, but which left the impression of sloppy work.

And don't be afraid to write notes to yourself. Jot down things to do, ideas, names of persons, facts to check. Keep a small notebook handy. Help yourself to remember details.

11. *Expect conflict and tension.*

By their very nature, public issues must be debated and are full of conflict. They involve many people and many interests, and they collide with each other. Thus the person who lives for moments of peace and harmony, at whatever cost, will be unprepared and won't have the toughness to hang in there, to stay in the arena of politics. Athletics is good training for politics. This is why I see my jogging as conditioning for my public work. I learned this the hard way. I began my political life as a person who preferred peaceful solutions. You don't always have to be a fighter yourself, but you have to be prepared to fight. Sometimes you have to be a referee, strong enough to pull the other fighters apart. At the same time, you've got to develop the tools to defend yourself. Once you have some scar tissues you won't bleed all the time. I am very serious about this. You can't pretend; this isn't just a pose. If you believe in something and if you want to accomplish something, you will have to be strong. If you need proof, just look at the great figures of history—from George Washington to Winston Churchill.

12. *Do a good job with what is in front of you today.*

Don't scheme and play games with your bosses (in my case, my "bosses" are the voters; in your case, they may be your teachers). I've spent a lot of time and mental energy unnecessarily. If you do good work on what is in front of you today, your future will take care of itself.

13. *Don't be in awe of high officials or leaders; they are people just like us.*

Every human being has his or her faults and limitations. Some have controlled and mastered their

Henry shares a happy moment with José Napoleón Duarte, President of El Salvador.

weaknesses better than others. And that's really why they have succeeded. Others give in to their limitations. Study what successful people have done. Admire and respect them but remember they are not superhuman and they don't always have superior abilities. What they have done, you can do.

14. *Every play counts the same in a game.* Have you ever noticed how a football team can often do things in the final two minutes of the game that it could not do before? That's when an earlier

"wasted play" may be needed. That's when previous mistakes are costly.

Or take baseball as another example. At the end of its season, a baseball team values each game when it's behind 1-1/2 games. Now it really matters to the team! But earlier in the season it wasn't watching that throw-away game. Perhaps the team lost a game when it made mistakes, or the concentration of the manager and the team just wasn't there. The truth is that the game it lost back there, early in the season, counts just as much in the standings as the game it needs two days before the end of the season. So watch for every opportunity. That's why some people think I am always working!

15. *Easing up can bring on a slump.*
The Detroit Tigers in 1984 started unbelievably fast and won the World Series; they never looked back. In 1985 they didn't get out to such a fast start and in June they fell behind to Toronto by just a game or two, and then, suddenly, they were behind by eight games. What does this tell us? Somewhere, back there in the early season, there was a game that was more than just a loss of a game. That loss turned into a slump when they lost eight out of ten. And at the end of the season the Tigers could look back and say "That's when we began our slump, that's when we lost our chance for

another pennant." That was the turning point. Don't let a slump—or a setback—become a habit. When you're in my position, you can't afford too many of them!

16. Assign work as much as possible, but be in charge.

You can't do everything, and shouldn't. Others can help you do more than you can alone. "Delegating" means assigning tasks. Match those tasks to the people. A task should never be more than a person can handle. People need to be challenged, but they also need to be satisfied and happy when they've finished a job. Set up a system of following up—or checking up—on your assignments to others. Tell your people about your plan to check on assignments. That way, there won't be any surprises. Be a good manager.

17. Respond quickly to opportunities.

You don't lose only by taking a step backward. You can also lose by failing to take a step forward, when it is there to be taken.

Hank Aaron is a good example of what I mean. He had a different way of approaching hitting than most players. He hit home runs by looking for the pitch he wanted, as opposed to just getting up there and hitting or taking a swing at whatever was thrown at him. He kept looking for a particular pitch. As a result, Hank Aaron often struck out without swinging, looking for a pitch that never came. But when he saw the pitch he wanted (his opportunity!), he was ready for it and he broke Babe Ruth's home run record.

Know what you are looking for. Take advantage of it when it shows up.

As mayor, I know what I want to accomplish for San Antonio. So when someone shows up at my office who has money to invest, or who has a plan for a factory my city needs—I see an opportunity because I already know how it fits into the big picture.

18. Get the job done.

No matter what it takes, do it. Some tasks require that you throw yourself into them, ignoring style, dress, grooming, niceties, and even the courtesies. When you peel everything away, what can you actually *do* at the very core of yourself? I've asked this question of myself in political campaigns, when I've been up against a wall. That's when you just dig down and find out what you're made of. I learned that at A&M—that there are some tasks that just require you to dive in and throw caution to the wind. Just do the job. Learn what you can do as a human being when you have exhausted all of your resources.

19. *Finish the job.*

Follow through. The difference between completing a job or not completing it can be measured, and it's the difference between night and day. You can't stop until the job is finished and it's up to acceptable standards. Later regrets are useless. That's something else I learned in college: when one was sent on a mission at A&M, the instructions were not to come back until it was done. That doesn't leave you much choice.

20. *Study your options (or choices) before making a decision.*

A politician has to consider the likelihood and price (or cost) of a decision, before taking some action. Here's an example from my home and family. I'm going to bed and suddenly wonder whether I locked the back door. The likelihood is that it is locked, because I do this regularly out of habit. However, my daughters are asleep in the next room. Their safety is the "price" that overrides "likelihood." So I get up and make sure that the back door is closed and locked. The stakes are so high that I take action. I want to be sure. On the other hand, in different situations, the price of a political decision is completely unacceptable when you think about the lives of children, damage to the environment, or the effects of nuclear war. You must weigh the risks when you make a choice.

21. *Know where you will take a stand.* It is very important to decide what should be first in your life, to believe in principles and values you will never compromise, and to be sure of the lines across which you will never step. What are you willing to fight for? Is there an issue or a principle for which you are willing to sacrifice everything? This is the stuff of character.

For me, one line I will not cross is anything that hurts the less fortunate in our society, anything that injures or threatens adults or children who can't help themselves. Another principle, for me, is democracy. That's why I had to add a little note to the Kissinger Report on Central America. I could go along with most of the report but I could not support aid to people who had previously worked for the Nicaraguan dictator Samoza.

22. *Move forward, even if you have to move slowly.* It's important to maintain a steady rate of speed toward progress. That means that when you have a goal for society, you just stay with it, even if setbacks require re-grouping. When you have a setback the only wise recourse may be small steps, but in the same direction. That is the way of civilized persons, to keep moving forward, guided by princi-

ples of what is right and just. I learned that lesson from Elliot Richardson. He was once betrayed by the White House on a piece of legislation. We went up to Camp David on a Saturday morning and he was trying to weigh the damage, asking himself, "Where do we go from here?" Should he drop the issue? Or should he re-group and start over again? Mr. Richardson decided the only way to act was to move forward and try again. For him, it was a matter of ethics, of doing the right thing. He would take small steps, but he would do his duty, and he would move ahead.

23. *Read the biographies of leaders.*

Study the lives of men and women from different periods and professions. There is much to be learned from leaders in the military, religion, politics, business, social movements, and the arts. You will discover that they are very human and very special. Their sense of personal destiny and their willingness to sacrifice will inspire and instruct you.

24. *Learn to appreciate that people are different and that everyone has something worthwhile to offer.* In the world in which you will grow up, things will be very different from what they are today. We must learn that differences among people are not based upon the color of their skin nor the language they speak—but upon what each person has to

offer. We will have to realize that we do not have all of the good ideas or the best ways of doing things. It is very important for you to learn at least one other language besides English—the more languages the better! Also, study all you can about the history and culture of other countries. This is the way we can appreciate and respect others, and be appreciated and respected by them.

Appendix A

An Early History of Texas and Mexico

Mexico shares more than 2000 miles (3200 kilometers) with the United States, yet many on both sides of the border know little about the history between the two neighboring countries. When America was a British colony, Mexico was a colony of Spain. Miguel Hidalgo y Costilla, a Mexican priest, sounded the cry for freedom from Spanish rule in 1810, and was executed by the Spaniards the following year. Mexico did not achieve its independence from Spain until 1821. As Mexico was liberated from Spain, its would-be liberators often became dictators. General Santa Anna, who fought the Texans at the Alamo, was one of these dictators.

At that time, Texas was a part of Mexico, though many U.S. citizens lived there. In 1835, the

Americans in Texas rebelled against the Mexican government and Santa Anna.

"Remember the Alamo!" is a battle cry first used by Texans and later by people all over the United States. In 1836 San Antonio's Alamo became famous as the site of the battle between the Mexican Army and people who wanted to separate Texas from the rule of Mexico. The fort was under seige for thirteen days, and 188 people were killed defending it.

Though Santa Anna won, the people did not give up. Texas finally won its independence from Mexico in the decisive battle at San Jacinto, led by Sam Houston. The victors formed the Republic of Texas, which included parts of what is now known as Colorado, Kansas, New Mexico, Oklahoma, and Wyoming. The victors never forgot the brave Mexicans and Americans who fought together to defend the Alamo, to fight tyranny, and to establish a new country of freedom and opportunity.

But the fighting was not over. In 1845 when Texas wanted to join the United States, Mexico still claimed Texas for its own. The United States declared war on Mexico. A treaty ended the Mexican War in 1848—Texas (and New Mexico and California) now belonged to the United States.

Benito Juarez, Mexico's first Indian president,

finally defeated General Santa Anna in 1855, and brought peace and freedom. Then the French invaded, establishing a monarchy in Mexico. This was followed by years of political confusion. A general named Porfirio Díaz overthrew the Mexican government and remained dictator for thirty-four years.

Some Mexicans fought for justice and democracy, including Francisco "Pancho" Villa, Emiliano Zapata, and Francisco Madero. Madero planned a successful revolution and was elected president in 1911, but he was assassinated by his enemies in 1913.

Henry Cisneros's grandfather, Rómulo Munguia, was arrested for supporting Madero, after Madero's death. Munguia's life was in danger, but he escaped to San Antonio, which had become a haven for many Mexican refugees who continued to work and plan for freedom in their homeland.

A new constitution was declared in 1917, but true reforms did not begin until Lázaro Cárdenas became president in 1934. Since his administration, there have been no revolutions in Mexico and its presidents serve a single term of six years.

(For more information about Mexico, read *Mexico: Giant of the South* by Eileen Latell Smith, also published by Dillon Press.)

Appendix B

Henry Cisneros: A Time Line

1947—Henry Gabriel Cisneros, born June 11, in San Antonio, Texas

1964—enters Texas A&M University

1968—receives bachelor's degree in English from Texas A&M; administrative assistant to the city manager, San Antonio and Bryan, Texas; commissioned officer in U.S. Army

1969—named assistant director of the Model Cities Department of San Antonio; marries Mary Alice Perez

1970—receives master's degree in urban and regional planning from Texas A&M; hired as administrative assistant to the executive vice-president, National League of Cities, Washington, D.C.; begins doctoral program at George Washington University

1971—first daughter, Teresa Angelica, is born; named White House Fellow, works as assistant to Elliot Richardson (secretary of the Department of Health, Education, & Welfare)

1972—Ford Foundation Research Grantee; enters John F. Kennedy School of Government, Harvard University

1973—appointed teaching assistant at MIT (Massachusetts Institute of Technology); receives master's degree in public administration from Harvard

1974—returns to San Antonio; named faculty member, University of Texas at San Antonio; receives doctoral degree in public administration from George Washington University

1975—elected to San Antonio city council; second daughter, Mercedes Christina, is born

1977—re-elected to city council

1978—resigns from U.S. Army Reserves with rank of captain

1979—re-elected to city council

1981—elected mayor of San Antonio

1982—selected as one of "Ten Outstanding Young Men of America" by U.S. Jaycees; Honorary Doctor of Laws degree, Texas Tech University

1983 re-elected mayor of San Antonio; Honorary Doctor of Laws degree, Incarnate Word College; Member, President Ronald Reagan's National Bipartisan Commission on Central America

1984—interviewed by Democrat Walter Mondale as possible vice-presidential candidate; Honorary Doctor of Laws degrees, George Washington University and Austin College

1985—re-elected mayor of San Antonio; joins faculty of Trinity University, San Antonio; Co-Chair, Texas Response to the 1985 Mexico City earthquake; Honorary Doctor of Laws degree, Claremont College

1986—Honorary Doctor of Humanities degree, Webster College; Honorary Doctor of Laws degree, City College of New York; Honorary Doctor of Humane Letters degree, Arizona State University

1987—re-elected mayor of San Antonio; first son, John Paul Anthony, is born; National Chairman, U.S. Savings Bonds for Cities; Honorary Doctor of Letters degree, State University of New York, Oneonta; Honorary Doctor of Laws degree, Amherst College

Bibliography

Anderberg, Ken. "Henry Cisneros: For Now, He's San Antonio's." *American City and County* (January, 1985).

Bell, Tom and Phelps, Christi. "The Shakedown." *San Antonio Monthly* (April, 1985).

Brenner, Anita. *The Wind That Swept Mexico.* Austin: University of Texas Press, 1971 (first published, 1943).

Diehl, Kemper and Jarboe, Jan. *Cisneros: Portrait of a New American.* San Antonio: Corona Publishing Co., 1985.

Emerson, Walter Caruth. *The Truth About Santa Anna.* Dallas: Cardinal Press, 1973.

Graves, Debbie. "Governor's Race Is Out for 1990, Cisneros Says." *Austin American-Statesman* (August 18, 1987).

Harrigan, Stephen. "Cisneros At Forty." *Texas Monthly* (September, 1987).

McNeely, Dave. "Cisneros Aims To Guard 8 Years Of San Antonio Development." *Austin American-Statesman* (March 25, 1987).

____. "Everyone Expects Cisneros To Run In '90—But For What?" *Austin American-Statesman* (March 26, 1987).

Nesmith, Samuel P. *The Mexican Texans.* San Antonio: Institute of Texan Cultures, 1981.

Pedersen, Daniel. "San Antonio: Putting Family First." *Newsweek* (September 14, 1987).

Pusey, Allen. "The Philosopher Mayor." *Dallas Morning News* (July 4, 1983).

Roberts, Naurice. *Henry Cisneros: Mexican-American Mayor.* Chicago: Children's Press, 1986.

Sills, Edward M. "Cisneros Backers Scouting Effects of Hobby Pullout." *San Antonio Light* (July 30, 1987).

Index